Jost thought this might
be useful my love — for the odd notes'.

XXXX

To our big cuddly Teddy'. X

Did you know that the teddy has been called the world's most popular soft toy? That in Britain, 63 houses out of every 100 have one? That there are more than 140 million of them in the USA?

– LEO ZANELLI

First published in Great Britain 1985 by Exley Publications Ltd., 16 Chalk
Hill, Watford, Herts, WD1 4BN. Copyright © 1983 by Running Press. This
British edition 1985 © Exley Publications Ltd. ISBN 1-85015-033-8 All rights
reserved. No part of this publication may be reproduced or transmitted in
any form or by any means, electronic or mechanical, including photocopy,
recording, or any information storage and retrieval system without permission
in writing from the publisher. Printed in Hungary by Kossuth.
Other notebooks in this series: A Hobbit's Journal, A Woman's Notebook,
The Cat Notebook.

TEDDY BEAR
JOURNAL

EXLEY PUBLICATIONS

It's hard to visualise the toys you had fifty years ago — all save Bear. He's as clear as if he were sitting on the desk in front of you. Of course . . . . he probably is.

– PAM BROWN
Writer and poet,
author of 'Mutterings of a Char'

Only a beast would trample bluebells or shoot a bird in flight.
Or burn a ted.

– HELEN THOMSON

Parents and others are very arbitrary in deciding when a child should stop having his or her teddy-bear around. My mother thought sixteen was about the right time. I still think she was wrong and I'm sure Theodore agrees with me.

– PETER BULL
Actor and writer,
author of 'Bear with me'

Someone should invent a harness in which to hang bears from the washing line. Pegs on the ears looks agonising.

– MARGOT BURNS

My Smokey the Bear has been dragged along carpets, dressed up in dolls' clothes and doctored with my plastic medical kit. He has sat on my bed in every house, flat and hostel I've lived in. When I had my tonsils out, he went to the hospital with me – all the way to the operating theatre. He has lost his belt, badge, shovel and hat. His fur is a little thin in places, but his dignity is still intact.

– JANE SELLMAN

Most toys you come across in jumble sales are worn-out playthings – the bears are abandoned friends awaiting rescue.

– PETER GRAY

It's hard to shut a toy box lid on a bear.

— PETER GRAY

It is astonishing, really, how many thoroughly mature, well-adjusted grown-ups harbour a teddy-bear — which is perhaps why they are thoroughly mature and well-adjusted.

– JOSEPH LEMPA

'And it's comforting to have something around that's lived with you all your life. And still likes you. There's nothing wrong with teddies for adults . . .'

– DR LEONARD KRISTAL
Publisher and psychologist

To a child, teddy is a bridge between a human being and an animal. He doesn't mind being taken for a walk, dressed in ridiculous hats, or even being read to. You can blame him for anything, and he won't deny it. His marvellous face expresses anything a child wants to feel or hear.

– PETER BULL
Actor and writer,
author of 'Bear with me'

Cuddly and warm, these calming creatures reassure me in the days of doubt when fears fly before reason and the world looms bleak instead of beautiful. The teddy-bear, all things to all ages, all sizes for all preferences, symbol that all is right with the world if one only believes.

– ANONYMOUS

I regret burning my old love letters and giving away my teenage records.
But it's Ted I miss most of all.

– WENDY FULLER

It's always a shock to discover in a bear's more intimate crevices the colour he used to be. Downright gaudy.

– PETER GRAY

There is a touch of sadness that endears bears to me, like layers of peeling paint on a beautiful old building. And there is a bear smell, musty, old and dry. It's the smell of an attic on a hot afternoon. Only good things that have lasted have that smell — trunks and lace and blankets.

– MICHELE DURKSON CLISE

*Now that I'm all grown up, I can buy any old teddy-bear I want
– except the old teddy-bear I want.*

– WILLIAM STERNMAN

'. . . the moment I unpack and put Theodore on my bedside table with his friends and props, the strange place becomes a sort of home. I think he's a symbol of unloneliness.'

– PETER BULL
Actor and writer,
author of 'Bear with me'

Teddies are father figures. To children they represent goodness, benevolence and kindliness. Parents who replace this cosy unharmful toy are a menace.

– JOSHUA BIERER, M.D.

A daughter leaving home packs Proust, the Pill and her teddy-bear.

– PAM BROWN
*Writer and poet,
author of 'Mutterings of a Char'*

I didn't know if my husband would understand about my teddy-bear, who's been sharing my bed since I was four. But they had a long talk and my husband discovered some things about Teddy that even I didn't know – like some nights Teddy would rather watch TV all night in the living room.

– LAURIE DILSON

'What sort of stories does he like?'
'About himself. Because he's that sort of Bear.'

– A. A. MILNE
Essayist and children's writer,
creator of 'Winnie-the-Pooh'

It takes a year of hard loving to run-in a bear.

– JAMES HACKETT

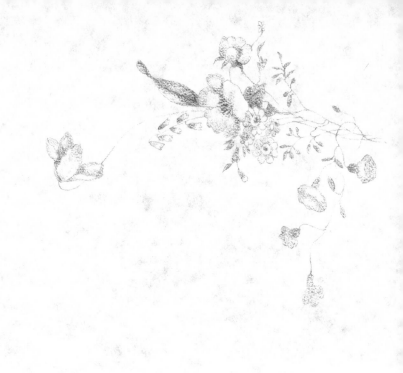

Wise teachers – well kind ones, anyway – invite teddies to school on the very first day.

– JAMES FURY

Teddy-bears are remarkably adaptable. How many other life forms can survive being kicked out of bed in the middle of the night, thrown in the washing machine with dirty socks, and fed a constant diet of Crayolas and Play-Doh?

– SARAH McCLELLAN

I was pushing my trolley down the supermarket aisle, mind focused on bananas and cereal, when I was distracted by a shelf of teddy-bears. One seemed to be reaching out to me. I looked at my shopping list, but there were no 'bears' written down – I try to avoid impulse buying – and carried on down the aisle. I suppose I needed that bear, because I wheeled my trolley around and in he went, sitting happily on a head of lettuce.

– MOLLY COURVILLE

A toy rabbit is an imitation rabbit.
A toy cat is an imitation cat.
A teddy-bear is himself.

– PAM BROWN
Writer and poet,
author of 'Mutterings of a Char'

As a speech therapist I scored over all the others in getting withdrawn, non-communicating children to talk. I fixed Ted straight in the eye and we'd carry on normal fluent conversation.

– HELEN THOMSON

His placid acceptance of everything and his serene composure, which has no smugness about it, can so often bring one's sense of proportion back and make one realise what are the important things in life and what aren't. For instance you can't imagine him running for a bus or a train or getting furious at the minor irritations and frustrations of modern living.

– PETER BULL
*Actor and writer,
author of 'Bear with me'*

A teddy may start off as a Popular Line — but soon becomes a comfortable eccentric.

– PETER GRAY

Love and loyalty are the bear essentials.
– MARIANNE PONTICIAN

One dreadful day
They hid him from me as a punishment:
Sometimes the desolation of that loss
Comes back to me and I must go upstairs
To see him in the sawdust, so to speak,
Safe and returned to his idolator.

– JOHN BETJEMAN

One day, when I was grown up and sad, I happened to meet Teddy in the attic. Suddenly the years dropped away and I felt young and loved again.

– HELEN FREISER

I can see a world without lots of things, but I can't see a world without teddy-bears.

– HARRY NIZAMIAN

How many children, do you suppose, have carried a lifelong resentment of parents responsible for the surreptitious removal of their teddy-bears?

– JOHN ZIFF

*Possession of a teddy-bear after a certain age
is a very private matter indeed.*

– PETER BULL
*Actor and writer,
author of 'Bear with me'*

My parents never forbad me my teddy-bear; I still have one. But what they did do was replace my old, worn-out cotton and wool bear with a sanitised nylon version. To this day, I have an ingrained aversion to change of any sort.

– MICHAEL CALLAGHAN

Why do people love teddy-bears? It's for their don'ts . . . they don't eat your food, they don't dance with your date, and they don't trump your ace lead.

— JIM DAVIS

It is most offensive to the kindly bears who've adopted us when we thoughtlessly blurt our some comment about 'real' bears, or 'live' bears, as if our very real and lively bear friends weren't.

– REV. ALLA BOZARTH-CAMPBELL

(My teddy-bear) is the physical proof and certain reminder of days that were made entirely for my enjoyment.

– PETER BULL
Actor and writer,
author of 'Bear with me'

A row of teddy-bears sitting in a toyshop, all one size, all one price. Yet how different each is from the next. Some look gay, some look sad. Some look standoffish, some look lovable. And one in particular, that one over there, has a specially endearing expression. Yes, that is the one we would like, please.

– CHRISTOPHER MILNE

Teddy-bears make great confessors, advisers, best friends – and scapegoats. Whenever my mother prepared to punish me for one misdeed or another, I would always be ready with 'Teddy did it'!

– ANONYMOUS

If the bear is missing an eye, and you can't find a replacement, make an eye-patch and your bear will look swashbuckling. If it is missing a paw or an arm, make a plaster cast and tell everyone that the arm was broken in a skiing accident.

– PEGGY BIALOSKY

Long before I grew up, my teddy-bear taught me what love really meant – being there when you're needed.

– JIM NELSON

My teddy was there when I had no friends to play with, no one to talk to, no one to share my little woes or my big joys. He looked constant and was constant. He never aged, no matter how tattered he became. His smell was the smell of my years as a boy, and he alone knew everything. Now, when I see him on the shelf, he is like my flesh and my soul – older, worn, but still full of happiness.

– ROBERT KUNCIOV

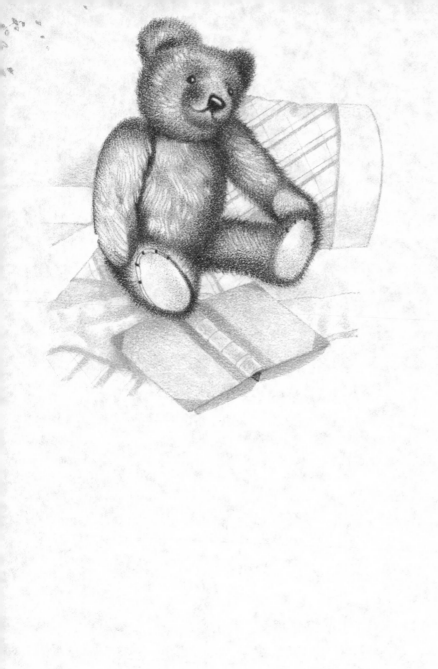

You know his eyes are coloured glass.
Then why does he look so desperately disconsolate when
you go out and leave him behind?

— PAM BROWN
Writer and poet,
author of 'Mutterings of a Char'

Learn to listen like a teddy-bear,
With ears open and mouth closed tight.
Learn to forgive like a teddy-bear,
With heart open, not caring who is right.
Learn to love like a teddy-bear,
With arms open and imperfect eyesight!

– SARAH McCLELLAN

Bears are irresistible because all people are kids. Grown-ups are just kids who have been around for a while (quite a while in some cases).

– KATHY CRESSMAN

When a child loves you for a long, long time, not just to play with, but REALLY loves you, then you become Real. Generally, by the time you are Real, most of your hair has been loved off, and you get loose in the joints and very shabby. But these things don't matter at all, because once you are Real, you can't be ugly – except to people who don't understand.

– MARGERY WILLIAMS